Contents

Woodlice

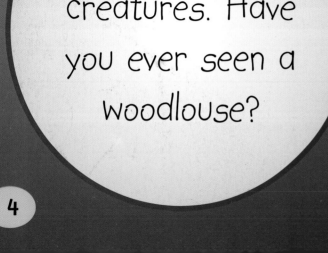

Woodlice are small creatures. Have you ever seen a woodlouse?

Creepy Creatures

Woodlice

Monica Hughes

Heinemann
LIBRARY

Little Nippers

www.heinemann.co.uk/library
Visit our website to find out more information about **Heinemann Library** books.

To order:
☎ Phone 44 (0) 1865 888066
▤ Send a fax to 44 (0) 1865 314091
▫ Visit the Heinemann Bookshop at www.heinemann.co.uk/library to browse our
   catalogue and order online.

First published in Great Britain by Heinemann Library, Halley Court, Jordan Hill, Oxford OX2 8EJ,
part of Harcourt Education. Heinemann is a registered trademark of Harcourt Education Ltd.

Designed by Jo Hinton-Malivoire and bigtop, Bicester
Models made by Jo Brooker
Originated by Dot Gradations
Printed by South China Printing Company, Hong Kong/China

ISBN 0 431 16303 0 (hardback)   ISBN 0 431 16308 1 (paperback)
06 05 04 03 02   06 05 04 03 02
10 9 8 7 6 5 4 3 2 1   10 9 8 7 6 5 4 3 2 1

British Library Cataloguing in Publication Data
Hughes, Monica
    Woodlice. - (Creepy creatures)
    1.Isopoda - Pictorial works - Juvenile literature
    I.Title
    595.3'72

Acknowledgements
The Publishers would like to thank the following for permission to reproduce photographs:
Heather Angel pp16, 20; Ardea: Jean-Paul Ferrero p23, Steve Hopkin pp4/5, 10, 17, 19, 22a, 22b;
BBC NHU: Dan Burton p21, Duncan McEwan p15; BBC NHU/Premaphotos p6; Bruce Coleman:
Dwight Kuhn pp12, 13; NHPA: NA Callow pp11, 14, Stephen Dalton p18; Oxford Scientific Films:
Scott Camazine p7, John Cooke pp8/9.

Cover photograph reproduced with permission of Ardea/Steve Hopkin.

Our thanks to Annie Davy for help in the preparation of this book.

Every effort has been made to contact copyright holders of any material reproduced in this book.
Any omissions will be rectified in subsequent printings if notice is given to the Publisher.

Looking for woodlice

Woodlice like dark and damp places.

You might see them at night
under logs or in dead leaves.

A woodlouse's body

A woodlouse has a hard body divided into lots of parts.
Can you count them?

Body parts

A woodlouse has seven pairs of legs.

antenna

It also has two antennae.

Young woodlice

A female woodlouse
lays her eggs.

Young woodlice have soft white
bodies but only six pairs of legs.

Growing up

As the woodlouse grows
it sheds the back half of
its shell first.

A few days later it
sheds the front half.

Food for woodlice

Woodlice eat dead plants as well as fungi and bark.

Sometimes they even eat the shedded skin of other woodlice!

Woodlice in danger

Frogs, lizards and hedgehogs all eat woodlice.

This woodlouse curls into
a ball when it is frightened.

Woodlice in winter

Woodlice do not move
around or grow in winter.

They hide under stones or logs
until the weather gets warmer.

Types of woodlice

There are about 40 different types of woodlice. They all look very much alike.

Woodlice are related to crabs and shrimps.

crab

shrimp

Index

The end

Notes for adults

This series supports the young child's exploration of their learning environment and their knowledge and understanding of their world. The four books when used together will enable comparison of similarities and differences to be made. (NB. Many of the photographs in **Creepy Creatures** show them much larger than life size. The first spread of each title shows the creature at approximately its real life size) The following Early Learning Goals are relevant to the series:
• Find out about, and identify, some features of living things, objects and events that they observe.
• Ask questions about why things happen and how things work.
• Observe, find out about and identify features in the place they live and the natural world.
• Find out about their local environment and talk about those features they like and dislike.

The books will help the child extend their vocabulary, as they will hear new words. Some of the words that may be new to them in **Woodlice** are *divided*, *pouch*, *fungi* and *antennae*. They may be surprised by the use of the words *woodlice* and *woodlouse* and might find it helpful to compare *mice* and *mouse*. Since words are used in context in the book this should enable the young child to gradually incorporate them into their own vocabulary.

The following additional information may be of interest:
Woodlice have existed since prehistoric times and are still found throughout the world. They take about two years to mature and live no longer than four years. A woodlouse's shell, which acts as good camouflage and protection, is constantly being shed. It must keep its shell damp at all times and so is found in damp places. It dies if its shell dries out. Woodlice feed mostly at night and as they eat rotting material they are good for the garden and improve the soil.

Follow-up activities
The child can record what they have found out about woodlice by drawing, painting, model-making, tape recording or writing.